Humpback Whale Tail • Photo © John Hyde/AlaskaStock Images

Inside Passage

Map

Southeast Alaska is known as the Inside Passage, a pristine land created by glaciers and covered in lush forests. The coastal communities of the Inside Passage reflect a region strong in Tlingit tradition. As the area is abundant in natural resources, the Tlingit people became skilled craftsmen and experts in the field of trade. From their coastal communities, they had free access to the sea and an overland route to the Interior. These routes were closely guarded and controlled by the Tlingits which enabled them to establish a trade empire.

The coastal communities also reflect a strong non-native influence. Foreign trade and exploration opened the way to foreign settlement. Dominant features found in the area include Russian Orthodox cathedrals, fish canneries, and the railroad, symbols of European and American expansion.

Ketchikan

Aerial view of downtown Ketchikan •
Photo by Joe Luman © Terrell Publishing Co.

"Thundering Wings" • Photo © Val McCown

Downtown Ketchikan •
Photo © Mark Kelley/AlaskaStock Images

Downtown Ketchikan • Photo © Clark Mishler/AlaskaStock Images

Inside Passage

Ketchikan

Misty Fjords • Photo © Mark Kelley/AlaskaStock Images

Centuries ago Tongass and Cape Fox Tlingit Indians established a fish camp along Ketchikan Creek, the "creek of the thundering wings of an eagle." During the mid 1880s, a Tlingit leader sold the present-day site of Ketchikan to a non-native who took advantage of the ample fish supply and opened the area's first fish cannery in 1886. Other settlers quickly moved in and also altered the Alaskan landscape with canneries and lumber mills.

Through totem poles, the Tlingit culture remains a prominent feature of the Ketchikan landscape. As home to the world's largest totem pole collection, these unique examples of native craftsmanship may be viewed at Totem Bight State Historical Park, Saxman Native Village, and the Totem Heritage Center Museum.

Located on the western coast of Revillagigedo Island, Ketchikan is the first port of call for northbound travelers. This southern city receives an annual precipitation of 165 inches, which many Ketchikan natives refer to as "liquid sunshine."

Totem Bight State Historical Park

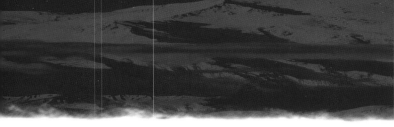

Ketchikan • Photo © Randy Brandon

Tlingit Family in traditional dress • Photo © Clark Mishler/AlaskaStock Images

Saxman Totem Park • Photo © John Warden/AlaskaStock Images

Bald Eagle •
Photo © John Hyde/AlaskaStock Images

Inside Passage

T ravel between coastal communities is hampered by the many islands, ice fields, and mountains that create the awesome Alaskan terrain. A state operated ferry, the Alaska Marine Highway System, connects the Inside Passage with British Columbia and Washington state. Weather permitting, ferry stops include intriguing and hard-to-reach ports, such as Wrangell and Petersburg.

Wrangell is Alaska's only city to have existed under four nations - Tlingit, Russia, Great Britain, and the United States. However, the Stikine Tlingits may not have been the first to inhabit the area. Ancient petroglyphs indicate people lived or passed through the area approximately 8,000 years ago.

Fishing enthusiasts find Wrangell and Petersburg to be ideal fishing sites. Brown and black bears favor Anan Creek near Wrangell. From the Anan Bear and Wildlife Observatory, visitors can watch the furry mammals catch upstream-bound salmon. Petersburg was named for a Norwegian immigrant, Peter Buschmann. After discovering ice from LeConte glacier was ideal for fish packing, Buschmann built a fish cannery in 1890. Because its population is primarily of Scandinavian origin, Petersburg is often referred to as "Little Norway."

Wrangell, Alaska • Photo © Mark Kelley/AlaskaStock Images

Petersburg, Alaska •
Photo © Jeff Gnass

Alaskan state ferry M/V MATANUSKA passes a commercial fishing boat •
Photo © Kim Heacox/Ken Graham Agency

Alaskan Black Bear - native of Southeast Alaska • Photo © Michael DeYoung/AlaskaStock Images

Inside Passage

Sitka

Sitka boat harbor with downtown and Mt. Edgecombe in background • Photo © Ernest Manewal/AlaskaStock Images

Overlooking the Pacific Ocean from the west side of Baranof Island lies the port of Sitka. Once home to a major tribe of Tlingits, the natives called their village Shee Atika. During the late eighteenth century, the Indians were displaced by Russian fur traders. The Russian-American Company established a base on Tlingit lands and renamed the village New Archangel. Unwilling to succumb to foreign rule, the Tlingits attacked and destroyed the Russian fort in 1802. Two years later, the Russians repaid the Tlingit action in kind at the Battle of Sitka, the Tlingits' last major stand against Russian rule. In 1808 New Archangel became the capital of Russian Alaska.

Although Sitka fell under the authority of the United States government in 1867, the influence of Russian culture is reflected in the local art, architecture, and celebrations. Housed at St. Michael's Cathedral is a significant collection of Russian Orthodox art and religious icons. A 1966 fire destroyed the original Russian cathedral that was constructed between 1844 and 1848.

St. Michael's Cathedral • Photo © Randy Brandon

This 1934 structure stands on the old Russian Parade ground. Elderly Alaskans live at the state owned home. • Photo © Randy Brandon

Dressed in authentic costumes, local women perform Russian dances. •
Photo © Kim Heacox/Ken Graham Agency

Aerial view of Sitka • Photo © Ken Graham/Ken Graham Agency

S i t k a

Sitka, Alaska •
Photo © Ken Graham/Ken Graham Agency

Bald Eagle • Photo © Cary Anderson/Ken Graham Agency

By the mid-1800s, Sitka was a major northern Pacific port. Although furs marked for European and Asian markets were the major export, other Alaskan resources such as salmon, lumber, and ice, made its way down the North American coastline to ports in California, Mexico, and Hawaii.

Following the 1867 Alaskan Purchase by the United States, the port community served as the territorial seat of government until 1906.

A fishing boat entering Sitka Sound off the coast of Baranof Island • Photo © Kim Heacox/Ken Graham Agency

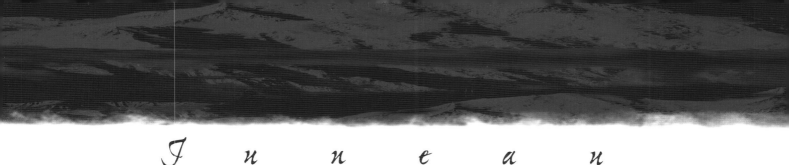

Juneau

Orca • Photo © Richard Johnson/AlaskaStock Images

Aerial view of downtown Juneau • Photo by Joe Luman © Terrell Publishing Co.

Governor's mansion in Juneau • Photo © Dan Hall

Alaska's seat of government moved from Sitka to Juneau in 1906. This city along the Gastineau Channel came into existence when Joe Juneau and Richard Harris discovered gold. In 1880 the pair struck a mother lode deposit, staked their claims, and developed the 160-acre town of Harrisburg. The area boomed. By the early 1900s, Juneau was the center of the world's largest mining operations. Deemed as nonessential to the effort, mining ceased in 1944 during World War II.

Although no longer haunted by miners, Juneau certainly remains a boom town. Annually Mendenhall Glacier, the Juneau Icefields, and other local sites attract close to 500,000 visitors.

Inside Passage

Juneau

St. Nicholas Russian Orthodox Church, Juneau, Alaska •
Photo © Jeff Schultz

Split Thumb above the Middle Branch of Norris Glacier •
Photo © Kim Heacox/Ken Graham Agency

Brown Bear Sow with Cub • Photo © Matthias Breiter/Ken Graham Agency

Mendenhall River and Glacier • Photo © Mark Kelley/AlaskaStock Images

Inside Passage

Juneau

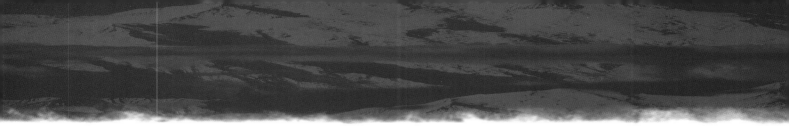

Mendenhall Glacier near Juneau • Photo © Kim Heacox/Ken Graham Agency

Inside Passage

Glacier Bay

In 1791 the British Admiralty ordered Captain George Vancouver to conduct a reconnaissance of the North American coastline stretching from California to Alaska. When the British explorer happened upon the area of present-day Glacier Bay in 1794, he noted that it was completely covered by ice. This massive sheet of ice was approximately 20 miles wide and extended to the St. Elias Mountain Range, a distance of more than 100 miles. Less than a century had passed when naturalist John Muir noted in 1879 that the tidewater glacier had retreated up the bay by 48 miles. By 1916, it had moved an additional 17 miles. This rapid movement has yet to be observed at any other location worldwide.

Situated along the border between Alaska and Canada, Glacier Bay National Park and Preserve is the site of the Brady Ice Field, one of three major ice fields in southeast Alaska. Originally established as a national monument in 1925, the ice field was designated as a National Park in 1980, a Biosphere Reserve in 1986, and a World Heritage Site in 1992.

Located within the park are twelve glaciers that calve into the bay. Glacier Bay National Park offers a glimpse of the Ice Age and is best observed by boat.

Alsek Glacier, Glacier Bay National Park • Photo © Fred Hirschmann/Ken Graham Agency

Reid Inlet, Glacier Bay • Photo © Randy Brandon

Riggs Glacier, Muir Inlet in Glacier Bay National Park • Photo © Fred Hirschmann/Ken Graham Agency

Black Bear Cub • Photo © Richard Moran/AlaskaStock Images

Humpback whale breaching • Photo © John Hyde/AlaskaStock Images

Inside Passage

Haines

Haines, with the Chilkat range in the background •
Photo © Ken Graham/Ken Graham Agency

Tlingit Indian Woman with ceremonial blanket • Photo © Clark Mishler/AlaskaStock Images

Chilkat Tlingit Indians called this area of the Inside Passage Dtehshus, meaning "end of the trail." During the mid to late nineteenth century few folks would have disagreed with the Indian name. Because the Chilkats controlled the major trade routes into Alaska's interior, travel to the region north of present-day Haines was hindered.

At the Chilkat's request, a Presbyterian minister built a mission and school at Dtehshus in 1881. The town of Haines developed around the mission. With the discovery of gold in the Klondike and the opening of the Dalton Trail, Haines became an important mining supply center for Yukon-bound prospectors. Haines was no longer the end of the trail, but a step forward for hopeful gold seekers.

Bald Eagles • Photo © Randy Brandon

Located approximately 20 miles from Haines is the Chilkat Bald Eagle Preserve. Created by the State of Alaska in 1982, the Preserve covers 48,000 acres and is home to the world's largest concentration of bald eagles.

Rafters on the Chilkat River with the Takhinsha Mountains in the background • Photo © Kim Heacox/Ken Graham Agency

Inside Passage

Skagway

Cruise ships docked at **Skagway Harbor** • Photo by Steve Gibson © Terrell Publishing Co.

Situated on the northernmost end of Lynn Canal, Skagway owes its very existence to the 1897 Klondike gold rush. Often referred to as the "Gateway to the Yukon," Skagway was characterized as a lawless society populated by con artists, thieves, and prostitutes who preyed upon the steady stream of prospectors headed for the gold fields of the Klondike.

The first non-native, Buddy Moore, settled here in 1887 and allegedly discovered the White Pass, a major route leading into the Yukon. In 1898 the pass became the site of Alaska's first railroad, the White Pass and Yukon Route Railroad. Today, visitors can ride the rails from Skagway's depot to the summit of White Pass and back.

Skagway Street Car on Main Street • Photo by Steve Gibson © Terrell Publishing Co.

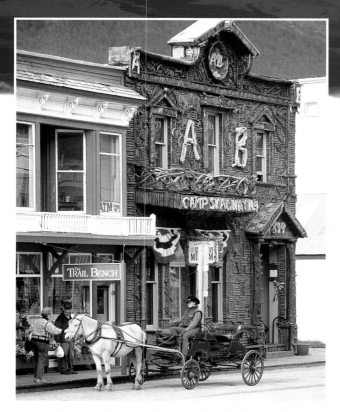

Horse Taxi Parked on Broadway Street in Historic Skagway
Photo © Mark Kelley/Alaska Stock Images

Chilkoot Trail - Skagway, Alaska
Photo © Bruce Herman/Alaska Stock Images

Aerial view of Skagway • Photo by Steve Gibson © Terrell Publishing Co.

Inside Passage

Skagway

White Pass Railway • Photo © Kim Heacox/Ken Graham Agency

White Pass & Yukon Route Railroad • Photo © Kim Heacox/Ken Graham Agency

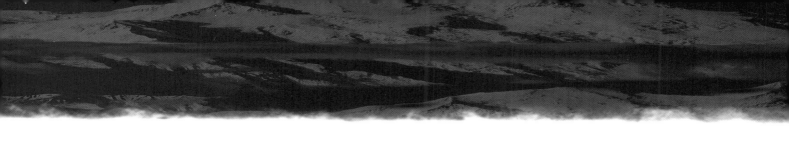

Wrangell Mountains • Photo © Ken Graham/ Ken Graham Agency

Worthington Glacier • Photo © Ken Graham/ Ken Graham Agency

Alaskan Forget-Me-Nots •
Photo © Ken Graham/ Ken Graham Agency

F a i r b a n k s

Fairbanks • Photo © Fred Hirschmann

Once home to the Koyukon Athabascan Indians, Fairbanks is today a modern city and the hub of Alaska's Interior region. As true of other frontier communities, Fairbanks began as a trading post. In 1901 Captain E.T. Barnette set up an establishment along the banks of the Chena River. Within a year the river's steamboat landing was teeming with gold seekers. A second wave of people crowded into the state's second largest city after a federal judge moved the seat of the Third Judicial District to Fairbanks in 1903.

The Alaska Territorial Legislature created in 1917 the Alaska Agricultural College and School of Mines. Today, the institution is better known as the University of Alaska. Although the main campus is located at Fairbanks, the university serves 113 Alaskan communities.

Aerial View of Griffin Park along the Chena River and Downtown Fairbanks
Photo © Fred Hirschmann

Riverboat "Discovery III" • Photo © Ken Graham/Ken Graham Agency

Bronze sculpture of "The Unknown First Family" • Photo © Ken Graham/Ken Graham Agency

Marker on the banks of the Chena River •
Photo © Ken Graham/Ken Graham Agency

Alaska

Musher Lorraine Temple with her dog team •
Photo © Ken Graham/Ken Graham Agency

Goldminers Yukon and Dexter Clark at the El Dorado Gold Mine •
Photo © Ken Graham/Ken Graham Agency

"Ice Fog" with a temperature of -42° • Photo © Arctic Circle Enterprises

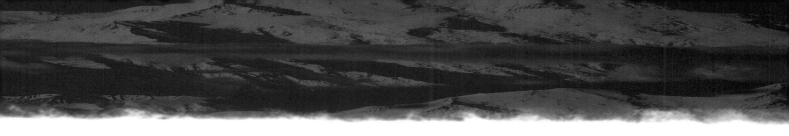

The climate of the Alaskan Interior is one of extremes. Temperatures range between -22° F to -2° F during the month of January alone; on occasion temperatures dip to a chilly -78° F. A common winter phenomena is known as ice fog. Because of frigid conditions, the fine particles of water suspended in the lower atmosphere that creates fog turns into ice. Therefore, ice fog is suspended ice particles!

Averaging four hours of daylight, winter days are short but far from dull. Sled dog races are a popular and typical week-end activity. Each February dog teams gather at Fairbanks for the popular 1,000 mile race from Fairbanks to Whitehorse in the Yukon.

Whereas winter is dark and cold, summer months are warm with long days. Between mid-May and early August the sun dips behind the horizon for a mere three hours, allowing the region and its people to bask in 21 hours of daylight. While summer temperatures soar to an average of 72° F, residents often picnic and pan for gold well past the midnight hour.

Moose antlers decorate a traditional food cache •
Photo © Steven Seiller/Ken Graham Agency

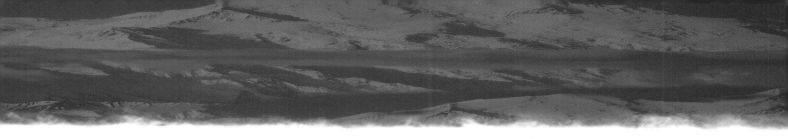

Land of the Midnight Sun • Photo © Arend-Soucek/AlaskaStock Images

Above the Arctic Circle

Northern lights with an igloo in the foreground • Photo © Daryl Pederson

An imaginary line 66½ degrees north of the equator marks the Arctic Circle. Beyond this northern boundary lies a land populated by an uncanny ancient people whose ancestors followed migratory animals across the Bering Land Bridge some 15,000 to 40,000 years ago. The Arctic Circle is also a place where the sun does not dip behind the horizon for one or more days in summer. It is a place where solar particles blown against the earth's magnetic field create an aurora across the dark winter sky.

The two largest cities in Alaska's Far North are Kotzebue and Barrow. Kotzebue is located 26 miles above the Arctic Circle and was once the hub of ancient trade routes. For at least 600 years, Inupiat Eskimos have resided in the Kotzebue area. Today, this Arctic city is home to one of the oldest and largest Inupiat Eskimo communities in North America.

Eskimo mother and girls • Photo © Randy Brandon

Eskimo blanket toss •
Photo © Clark Mishler/
AlaskaStock Images

Situated along the Chukchi Sea coast, Barrow is the northernmost community in North America. Residents here experience the phenomenon of the midnight sun between mid-May and early August. During this period the sun is a constant fixture in the sky and a time for celebration. A traditional Eskimo game enjoyed at various sun festivals is the blanket toss, a lively activity which owes its origins to hunting. Using a large skin, a hunting party would toss a member into the air, thus providing the hunter an unobstructed view of the Arctic terrain.

With the arrival of spring, all living things, man and animal alike, emerge from their winter homes. Polar bears return to the Arctic coast in search of seals, walrus, and other marine mammals. Although polar bears are a protected species, Eskimos are permitted to hunt these large members of the bear family.

Polar Bear • Photo © Gary Schultz/AlaskaStock Images

Aleutian Islands

Alaska brown bears with sockeye salmon • Photo © Kim Heacox/Ken Graham Agency

Holy Ascension Russian Orthodox Church • Photo © Ken Graham/Ken Graham Agency

S ituated at the end of the Aleutian Chain, the Dutch Harbor and Unalaska vicinity was once home to more than 1,000 Aleuts highly skilled in the art of fishing and fur trapping. Because of its natural barriers and location, Dutch Harbor became, and remains, a popular port along the Pacific Rim trade route. A Russian fur trading port was established on the island in 1768. The Russian Orthodox Church of the Holy Ascension of Christ was constructed in 1825 and is the oldest Russian Orthodox cruciform-style church in North America.

Unalaska is in the foreground with the port of Dutch Harbor in the background •
Photo © Barbara Keller

Alaskan Sockeye salmon • Photo © Jeff Foott

Alaka

Kodiak

odiak Island, often referred to as the "emerald isle," is Alaska's largest island and the second largest in the United States. The Sugpiaq Eskimos are native to the island and have dwelled here for more than 8,000 years. After European contact in the mid-eighteenth century, the large Eskimo population dwindled and their culture neared extinction.

Present-day Kodiak is the site of the first Russian colony established in North America. Prior to its relocation to Sitka, the city of Kodiak served as the first capital of Russian Alaska.

A familiar island dweller is the Kodiak brown bear. Approximately 3,000 of these bears live at the 1.9 million-acre Kodiak National Wildlife Refuge, which encompasses two-thirds of Kodiak Island and a portion of Afognak, a neighboring island. With a height of over 11 feet and weight in excess of 1200 pounds, these bears are the largest carnivores in the world.

Kodiak brown bears •
Photo © Don Pitcher/AlaskaStock Images

Kodiak, Alaska • Photo © Jeff Gnass

Kenai Peninsula

Homer

Homer, Alaska and Kachemak Bay • Photo © Randy Brandon

Bald Eagles • Photo © Cary Anderson/Ken Graham Agency

Homer, Alaska • Photo © Jeff Schultz/AlaskaStock Images

The Kenai Peninsula community of Homer lies on the north shore of Kachemak Bay. Originally a nineteenth-century coal mining town, Homer has since become famous for sport fishing. Dubbed the "Halibut Fishing Capital of the World," Homer is the site of the annual Jackpot Halibut Derby. Homer is also famous for its spit, a 4½ mile long point of land covered in gravel and sand that juts into the bay.

Kenai Peninsula

Mt. Redoubt • Randy Brandon

Connected to the mainland by a narrow isthmus, this southcentral peninsula is a medley of natural wonders. Snowcapped mountains dominate the eastern landscape. In contrast, low rolling hills, carpeted with deciduous forests that descend into the waters of Cook Inlet, characterize the west. Crystalline rivers and lakes teeming with king salmon, rainbow trout, and Dolly Varden criss-cross the peninsula's width.

During the early 1800s, Russian settlers established the community of Ninilchik along the western coast. An old Russian church and cemetery is among the few surviving structures that date back to the town's origin. Across Cook Inlet an active volcano range runs along Ninilchik's opposing shore. Mt. Redoubt stands as proof of the fiery ring beneath the Pacific Ocean.

Kenai Lake • Photo © Ken Graham/Ken Graham Agency

Fisherman's Paradise •
Photo © Ken Graham/Ken Graham Agency

Historic Russian church in Ninilchik • Photo © Peter Lik

Kenai River • Photo © Tom Walker

Kenai Peninsula

Seward

Aerial of a cruise ship at dock in Seward with Mt. Marathon beyond •
Photo © Ken Graham/Ken Graham Agency

Exit Glacier • Photo © Randy Brandon/AlaskaStock Images

Sea Otter • Photo © Leo Keeler/Ken Graham Agency

Along the Kenai Peninsula's southeast coast lies the port city of Seward. The city is situated on Resurrection Bay at the base of Mt. Marathon. As is true of Resurrection Bay, place names and the stories attached are often as intriguing as the site itself.

While sailing from Kodiak, a sudden storm forced the Russian fur trader Alexander Baranof and his crew to seek shelter along an unfamiliar coast. Baranof happened upon a bay and aptly named it Resurrection because the discovery was made on the Russian Sunday of the Resurrection. The city of Seward bears the name of the man who negotiated the Alaskan Purchase, William Seward.

Kenai Fjords

Seward is often described as the gateway to Kenai Fjords National Park. Established in 1980, the park encompasses 580,000 acres of coastal wilderness. Within the park boundaries lies the Harding Ice Field. Evidence suggests that this 300-square-mile ice field may be a rare example of the Pleistocene ice masses which covered an ancient Alaska. This frozen mass is the source of more than 40 glaciers. As the glaciers retreated away from the shoreline, a land marked with fjords and lush forests was left in their wake.

An array of Alaskan wildlife are attracted to and live around the rugged coastline. Mountain goats clamor along the rocky edges, while sea otters claim the bays and lagoons. During the summer months, harbor seals can be seen sunning on newly calved icebergs. A large number of birds, including bald eagles and puffins, annually return to the fjords to nest and raise their young.

Horned puffins •
Photo © Didier Lindsey/Ken Graham Agency

Kenai Fjords • Photo © Ken Graham/Ken Graham Agency

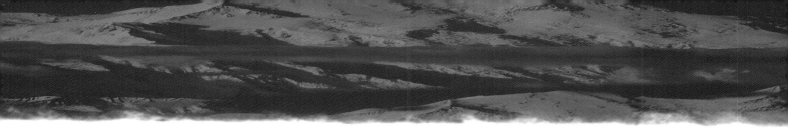

Kenai Fjords • Photo © Ken Graham/Ken Graham Agency

Alaska

Portage Glacier

Portage Glacier •
Photo © Allen Prier/Ken Graham Agency

Portage Glacier flowing into Portage Lake •
Photo © Kim Heacox/Ken Graham Agency

The Begich Boggs Visitors Center •
Photo © Gene Jansen/Ken Graham Agency

Situated in the Portage Valley region of the Chugach National Forest, the site of Portage Glacier and Portage Lake is among Alaska's top ten attractions. Centuries ago folks used Portage Glacier as an overland route between Cook Inlet and Prince William Sound. During the early 1900s, the beginnings of Portage Lake was discovered after the glacier had receded by more than two miles.

Portage Valley is also the site of the Begich Boggs Visitor Center, a center staffed by individuals dedicated to the explanation of glacial activity. Visitors flock to Begich Boggs not only to view the valley's seven glaciers, but also to observe towering icebergs floating in Portage Lake.

Byron Glacier • Photo © Ken Graham/Ken Graham Agency

Explorer Glacier • Photo © Ken Graham/Ken Graham Agency

Alaska

Mt. Alyeska

One of the first recorded gold strikes in Alaska occurred in the Girdwood Valley. The Aleutian people referred to this region as Alyeska or "great land." Most Alaskans would agree that Mt. Alyeska is indeed a great land, even a golden land. In fact, it is one of the few places in the world where snow skiers can observe the rolling of the ocean while gliding down the slopes. As the largest year-round resort in the state of Alaska, Mt. Alyeska and the Girdwood Valley offer visitors a wide range of recreational activities which includes fishing, hiking, canoeing, mountain climbing, and snow skiing. At a height of 3,939 feet, Mt. Alyeska offers a spectacular view of the valley and the community of Girdwood. Rather than scale the towering mountain, most folks reach their destination by chairlift. Rising 2,000 feet above the valley floor, the mile-long chairlift travels three-fourths of the way to the mountain's peak.

Mt. Alyeska Ski Resort •
Photo © Ken Graham/Ken Graham Agency

Mt. Alyeska Ski Resort, Girdwood, Alaska • Photo © Ken Graham/Ken Graham Agency

Northern Lights over Mt. Alyeska • Photo © Randy Brandon

Mt. Alyeska Resort tram with the town of Girdwood in Glacier Valley • Photo © Ken Graham/Ken Graham Agency

Alaska

Turnagain Arm

Turnagain Arm • Photo © Ken Graham/Ken Graham Agency

Turnagain Arm • Photo © Randy Brandon

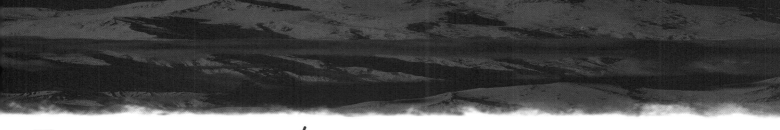

Anchorage

Mt. Susitna • Photo © Gene Jansen/Ken Graham Agency

While searching for a Northwest Passage that would link the Pacific and Atlantic Oceans, the British sea captain James Cook sailed up an unfamiliar waterway, now known as Cook's Inlet. He set anchor in a low lying area surrounded by two arms of water and a mountain range. The southern arm of water Cook dubbed "River Turnagain," which is the action Cook ordered upon departure - the ship turned around. On a visit to the region in 1794, Captain George Vancouver renamed the river, calling it Turnagain Arm.

Anchorage, Alaska • Photo © Ken Graham/Ken Graham Agency

Alaska

Anchorage • Photo © Ken Graham/Ken Graham Agency

Anchorage

Town Square Park, Anchorage • Photo © Ken Graham/Ken Graham Agency

The state's largest city, Anchorage, owes its birth to the railroad. In order to transport coal from Alaska's interior to the lower 48 states, a railroad connecting the coal fields to an ice-free port was essential. Therefore, in 1914 Congress signed into law the Alaska Railroad Act, which created the only railroad owned and operated by the federal government. The proposed route, selected by President Woodrow Wilson in 1915, passed through an area known as Ship Creek. News of the railroad spread throughout the area. Hundreds of people seeking employment opportunities converged upon the tiny community. The railroad not only created jobs, it created a new city. In April 1915 a post office was established and Ship Creek was renamed Anchorage.

Today, Anchorage is a modern urban city and serves as the hub of Alaska's commerce sector. With over 162 parks, a variety of recreation facilities, and the Alaska Center for the Performing Arts, the folks of Anchorage are able to experience the splendor of the last frontier in a metropolitan setting.

Anchorage, Alaska • Photo © Jeff Schultz/Alaska Stock

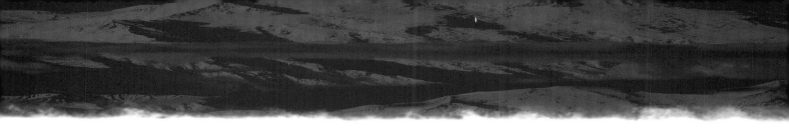

Alaska Center for the Performing Arts • Photo © Bruce M. Herman

Float plane flies off into the sunset • Photo © John Warden/AlaskaStock Images

Alaska

Matanuska Valley

Matanuska Valley • Photo © Ken Graham/
Ken Graham Agency

Palmer, with the Matanuska River flowing past • Photo © Ken Graham/Ken Graham Agency

Willow Ptarmigan - Alaska's State Bird • Photo © Jeff Gnass

Matanuska Glacier • Photo © Ken Graham/Ken Graham Agency

Denali National Park

On February 26, 1917, 1.9 million acres of Alaskan wilderness was designated as a wildlife refuge designed to protect large animals native to the region such as Dall sheep, caribou, moose, grizzly bears, and wolves. In addition to the wildlife population, the park possessed another fascinating feature - the tallest mountain in North America. Mt. McKinley National Park, named in honor of President William McKinley, was incorporated into Denali National Park in 1980.

Wild and unspoiled, the 6 million-acre park is the epitome of America's last great frontier. To a degree, a visit to Denali National Park is a step into the past. The towering peaks of the Alaska Range are visible signs of tectonic plate activity, the violent crashing and rubbing of the earth's crust. Glacial movement smoothed the rubbles of rock into mountain slopes and valleys. Deciduous forests stand along young glacial streams. More than 430 flowering plant species grace both mountain and valley, while providing the wildlife population food. This is a land that demands respect, but permits visitors to experience nature's awesome wonders.

Denali National Park • Photo © Ken Graham/Ken Graham Agency

Denali Visitor Center •
Photo by Joe Luman © Terrell Publishing Co.

Rafting on the Nenana River in Denali National Park • Photo © Kim Heacox/Ken Graham Agency

Denali Visitor Center •
Photo © Ken Graham/Ken Graham Agency

Caribou • Photo © Didier Lindsey/Ken Graham Agency

Talkeetna • Photo by Joe Luman © Terrell Publishing Co.

Talkeetna • Photo by Joe Luman © Terrell Publishing Co.

Talkeetna • Photo by Joe Luman © Terrell Publishing Co.

Alaska Railroad • Photo © John Warden/AlaskaStock Images

Photo by Joe Luman © Terrell Publishing Co.

Denali National Park offers a wide range of visitor use which includes wildlife viewing, mountaineering, backpacking, and rafting. For those who wish to view the splendor, but not conquer the terrain, may do so by shuttle bus or train. Whatever mode of transportation or activity is elected, all park visitors are encouraged to make the Visitor Center their first stop. Updated park information is an essential ingredient to an enjoyable experience. The quaint town of Talkeetna offers a dramatic view of the mountain from the south side.

Denali National Park

Mt. McKinley

Moose in Wonder Lake, Denali National Park • Photo © Randy Brandon

Moose •Photo © Steven Nourse/Ken Graham Agency

Toklat River • Photo © Ken Graham/Accent Alaska

Dall Sheep • Photo © Howie Garber/Ken Graham Agency

The Athabascan Indians called the massive peak Denali or "High One." At 20,320 feet, Mount McKinley is indeed the "High One" on the North American continent. This towering member of the 65 million-year-old Alaska Range is the result of the Denali Fault, which stretches 1,300 miles from the Yukon border to the Aleutian Peninsula. The first expedition to conquer the mountain's southern summit, the true summit, took place on June 7, 1913, and was led by Harry Karstens and Hudson Stuck. Since that historic moment, mountaineers continue in the quest to conquer the "High One."

Mt. McKinley • Photo © Jeff Schultz/Alaska Stock

Denali National Park

Mt. McKinley

Mt. McKinley • Photo © Jeff Gnass

Denali National Park

Gray Wolf • Photo © Denver Bryan